IN PRAI!

PASTORAL MENTORSHIP, HUMILITY, AND
THE DANGERS OF YOUTH

IN PRAISE OF OLD GUYS

PASTORAL MENTORSHIP, HUMILITY,
AND THE DANGERS OF YOUTH

by

Nicolas Alford

and

Nicholas Kennicott

WRATH AND GRACE PUBLISHING
COLUMBUS, GA

For Dad—The best old guy I could ever want in my life. Thanks for always being around and never giving up on me. I love you, dad.

For Nicholas, Jr.—I hope you will one day be a wise, godly old guy and I hope to help you get there, despite my weaknesses, by the grace of God. I love you, son.

—Nick Kennicott

This book is dedicated to all my old guys: a pile of Baptists; a smattering of Presbyterians; a few who proudly defy classification; two grandfathers; a brother; and (before them all) one father – who remains the definition of the best that word can mean.

I learned from all of you, even when you didn't know you were teaching. Thank you.

And to Shelby, of course.

—Nicolas Alford

Table of Contents

Acknowledgments   ix

Foreword   xvii

Preface   xxi

Chapter One: Talking 'Bout My Generation   1

Chapter Two: Age Is More Than A Number   11

Chapter Three: More Whips! More Scorpions!   19

Chapter Four: Despicable Youth   27

Chapter Five: Like Father, Like Son   37

Chapter Six: In Praise Of *Really* Old Guys   49

Conclusion: *Go West Young Man*   65

Appendix: Suggested Reading   75

Acknowledgments

I am very thankful to have had the opportunity to work on this project with one of my best friends in life and ministry, Nicolas Alford. While our journeys into pastoral ministry are very different, those differences have given both of us a unique desire to see other young pastors do what we did well and avoid all the things we did wrong. Most of the things done wrong are on my side of the equation, and I've praised God for the many things I've been able to learn from my friend. Putting one's name next to mine in print is a risky thing, so I don't take Alford's willingness to work with me lightly.

Writing a book of this nature simply takes time and experience, and none of that time nor those experiences would've been possible without a patient, loving, and forgiving local church. I cannot say enough good things about Redeemer Baptist Church and the people God has given me the opportunity to pastor. They put up with me in my twenties and continue to push me to be a better man, a better pastor, and a better leader each and every day. RBC gave me several opportunities for writing leave and regularly checked on the progress of the work. I know I am able to do what I do because I am loved and prayed for by the people of God.

I give thanks to God for the old(er) guys in my life who have taught me, challenged me, pushed me, and encouraged me along the way. Chaplains Col. Dave Bowlus and Maj. Mark Winton who encouraged me while I was in the Army and beginning my pursuit of ministry; Dr. J. Calvin Webb for taking me under his wing and licensing me to preach; Pastor Devin Bell for always being a friend and mentor, and a voice of sound wisdom when things were difficult; Pastor Murray Brett for always taking a great interest in me, my family, and the ministry at RBC—he has pushed me to think deeper and more biblically about the things that matter most in the Christian life as I pursue communion with God; Bob Selph for never being afraid to tell young men when we're not being wise, for actively displaying what it means for a pastor to "do the work of an evangelist" and for always doing what he does with a loving heart and a big smile; Gordon Taylor for sage wisdom and advice and a constant willingness to come alongside and encourage pastors and churches to keep pressing on toward the great Celestial City; Pastor Wayne Brandow, a hero to me for serving the same small church in a small town since he was

25 years old, never giving up even when most people would think it reasonable; Pastors David Campbell, Baruch Maoz, Donnie Martin, Conrad Mbewe, and Robert Elliot for your friendship, encouragement, and valuable feedback on this project; Pastor Tracy Sullens, Pastor James Eady, Pastor Chris Okogwu, Pastor Nick Batzig, the Bacon Brothers (you know who you are), Olamide Bode Falase, and Joel Blaxland for being amazing and godly friends, even though I'm pretty bad at being a friend; And my co-elders, Russ Jenkins, Jeff Stephens, and Sam Barber (NOT older) for keeping me accountable, praying for me, and trusting me.

Of course, the first old guy in my life is my dad—a natural leader who taught me the value of hard work, generosity, and making sure I have the right priorities in life. My parents have encouraged me in whatever I've done and have never quit being dependable and involved. God blessed me with amazing parents that I love very much.

My wife and three children are patient and loving in ways I could never describe. I'm not delusional to think I'm anything other than a difficult man, but they love me anyway. In my opinion, I'm blessed beyond all men—they teach me more about myself than I could ever learn otherwise and they bring joy indescribable into my every day.

I want to thank Wrath and Grace for taking a chance on two young guys and allowing our voices to be heard. May the Lord be pleased to use it for his glory and the good of his Church.

—Nick Kennicott

* * * * * * * *

Writing these acknowledgments after Kennicott has already finished his puts me at a disadvantage. Not only has he set the bar irresponsibly high, he has stolen all the best words. Still, I'll see what I can whip up with the leftovers.

Perhaps one small failure of our book is that we never quite define *old guy*. We rhapsodize on about gray hair, baldness, and mauling by bears (which, incidentally, was the moment I believe we won over Luke Walker), but the adjective itself remains a bit abstract. As a remedy to that omission (and with an ulterior motive to be revealed below), I'll simply say that the *old guys* we're praising are those men of godly character further along in life, stopping and turning to lend a hand.

By that standard, where do I start? The Lord has particularly lavished this blessing into my life. It begins at home, of course, and that begins with Dad. My father showed me that true integrity is never incompatible with loving care, and that strength is something you don't have to talk about if you actually have it. I think I was primed to praise old guys because I had the best one right in front of me. Add an older brother to look up to and I was sold. My two grandfathers (one a Deputy-Sheriff-Cowboy-Marine with a spark in his eye, hymn in his heart, and fierce love for family; the other the best fishing partner and spiritual example for whom a grandson could hope) only added to the blessing and the lesson of learning from the old guys. And although not all the lessons I learned being raised on job sites in the Pacific Northwest would have necessarily thrilled my mother, I love all those crusty old guys with all my heart.

In ministry, I couldn't list all the faithful pastors, the volunteers, and the summer camp leaders without being terrified that I would omit someone critical. So let me just name a few names, with the understanding that surely I can't name them all: Tom Collins, Guy Smith, Ben Selph, Bob Selph, Bob Gonzales, Greg Nichols, Scott Van Steenburgh, Brian Smith, and Jamie Howell. Out of these, I have to highlight Guy Smith and Bob Selph for pouring an unusual amount of pastoral attention and assistance into a young knucklehead like me. You have no idea how much it means.

Time to reveal my ulterior motive in the above definition of an old guy: if an *old guy* is just a man of godly character further ahead in life who stops to turn and lend a hand, Nick Kennicott is one of mine. You don't have to be that much older in years (although he's got me beat by a few months) to be older in life and accrue a surplus of wisdom to share. Nick, thank you for your friendship in life, your example in ministry, your courage to serve, your assistance in growth, and your partnership in this project (plus whatever else we get around to actually finishing). I'm so thankful for you, brother.

After Christ, the best gift the Father of Lights ever gave me was my wife and kids. Shelby, Madelyn, Jackson, Jacob – I could puzzle out a million ways to write it and still come back to this: I love you. More than I knew a heart could love, I love you.

Deepest thanks to Grace Baptist Church of Taylors for your loving support and gracious patience. It has been my joy to live out the story of this book in your midst.

Thank you to Free Grace Baptist Church for letting a young man grow up into ministry and for your sacrificial support and prayer.

Wrath and Grace, it is an honor to publish this under your name and a privilege to stand with you for Christ.

Conrad Mbewe, thank you for embodying the idea of this book in your own life and ministry, and for writing such a pitch-perfect foreword.

Above all, we both acknowledge Jesus Christ. More than mere acknowledgment, we cast whatever crowns our prideful hearts may hoard down before his glorified feet.

May he increase, and we decrease.

—Nicolas Alford

Foreword

I've been there, done it, and am very embarrassed about it. God have mercy! Thankfully, whereas it cost many other young pastors their pastorates, I survived to tell the story. And the story is quite simple: "I should have listened to the wisdom of the sages."

That is what this book is all about. I wish it had come out a little earlier—say, thirty years ago. Having said that, I suspect I would not have heeded its counsel then…until it was too late. Is that not one of the occupational hazards of youth? We listen too little too late.

We are so easily enamoured by apparent success, especially when sleek young pastors wearing designer clothes and being thronged by crowds are the ones telling us they have finally found the formula for success. We do not realise that this is nothing more than the crackling of thorns in the fire—very noisy but does not last long and cannot cook a real meal! Let us not be fooled. There were similar "sleek young men" a generation ago and they should serve as scarecrows to us today, if only we can listen to those who watched them rise and fall with a thud. There is nothing new under the sun. Not all that glitters is gold.

There is a stabilising panoramic view of life that God only gives those who have walked long and hard in this life. Faith has been augmented by sight. This is what David referred to in his famous psalm against fretting. He wrote, "I have been young, and now am old, yet I have not seen the righteous forsaken or his children begging for bread" (Psalm 37:25). Therefore, David seems to be saying, fretting is useless. Put your trust in God.

It is often the anxieties of youth that cause us to make decisions that we later regret. Listening to those who have trodden the path we are in much longer than we have will save us from those anxieties. Jesus Christ is the same yesterday, today, and forever (Heb. 13:8). If only Rehoboam, the son of Solomon, had realised this, the story of Israel as a nation would have been altogether different.

This book goes further than urging us to sit at the feet of the living old guys. The authors call our attention to the classics, to those books that were written by authors who have long been gathered with their fathers but that have stood the test of time. Like the writing of hymns and songs of worship, each generation will have plenty of them written down but few of them make it to the next generation. The few that do so often make it because they are of high quality and they strike a deep chord in the hearts of God's people. That is how it is with books that have become classics. I cannot emphasise enough the need for our younger pastors to not only read the latest books but to also drink from the old wells. The books that have stood the test of time strike a deep chord in our hearts.

I am glad that Nicolas Alford and Nicholas Kennicott have put into print what most of us only think about with regret. Although most illustrations relate to the American culture, the principles are applicable anywhere. We now have the opportunity to put a small book into the hands of younger men training for the ministry or starting out in ministry that not only spells out the danger of youthful pride but also points where the counsel of the sages can be found.

I will be putting this book into the hands of our pastoral students and interns with a warning that only pride will keep them from heeding the counsel that is found in these pages and that "God opposes the proud but gives grace to the humble" (1 Peter 5:5). Hopefully, we will see less aborted pastorates by doctrinally sound men. This can only result in steady pastorates whose longevity will result in sound churches that will impact society for the glory of

God. This book may be small but its potential for good is incalculable.

—Dr. Conrad Mbewe

Preface

If you've ever wondered who it is, I am the guy for whom the moniker "know-it-all" was invented. And while I didn't realize it—and even if I did I wouldn't have admitted it—for many years of my life I was always certain I was the smartest guy in the room. If I wasn't the smartest guy, I was willing to go toe-to-toe with him, even if that meant faking it along the way. There's nothing like self-assurance to put you at the top of your peer group before you're ready. There's nothing like pride to put you in a place where those who have gone before you and walked in shoes you'll never fit don't really mean a whole lot. Guys like me have a knack for covering up a shortage of wisdom with the ability to make others feel inferior, to know *just enough* to sound intelligent, and to direct a conversation as to never walk too near those things we have yet to learn about on our own. Admitting a lack of knowledge to learn from someone else is out of the question.

I recently turned 36 and have been reminded of something very important yet again: it's the old cliché—the more I know, the more I realize I don't know. I wish I had learned this earlier in life; it would have saved me from a lot of uncomfortable, sinful, foolish situations. But I'm also a strong believer in the sovereignty of God and have full assurance that all things will come to pass by the divine decree of God for my good, and for his glory. Those times of my life have prepared me to be a better Christian, a better husband, a better father, a better pastor, and a more humble author of a book of this nature.

I have been a pastor now for 11 years, and in that time I have endured some difficult circumstances that have brought me low. I have been the pastor at Redeemer Baptist Church in Rincon, Georgia for 10 years. We went through a difficult and sad split 2 years into my post. And if you're doing pastor math, my first ministry position lasted exactly 1 year to the day. It was a combination of a guy who shouldn't have been ordained yet (me) and a congregation that was not overly fond of a certain kind of theology and practice. I don't resent or regret any of the experiences or people I've encountered in pastoral ministry. The Lord has used all my experiences to bring me to the end of myself, to make me all the more aware of my pride, and to alert me to the need for older men of wisdom in my life. I'm thankful for old guys who can rebuke, encourage, and direct me in the ways of life and ministry that are best arrived at through the school of hard knocks (they have earned many a PhD from this prestigious learning institution).

When Alford (who, by the way, spells his first name completely wrong) first wrote a blog post entitled, "In Praise of Old Guys" I was reminded of all the books I've read, conferences I've attended, and conversations I've had with guys in ministry who were and are a lot like I was, and in some ways still am. The luddites and fuddy-duddies just don't get it, and the church needs us more than anything— she needs a rescue, and God was gracious enough to give our generation of pastors to be her prince. Unfortunately we've forgotten that the Church already has a monarch (and we're not Him).

I now have several older men in my life that I turn to on a regular basis. They are of incalculable value to me and I trust that I am a better man because of them. By God's grace I hope to share with you what I've learned, and pray that if you're a young Timothy you will find a Paul or two along the way, and if you're an old guy, you will share your wisdom with guys like us—*we need you.* We're not as wise as we think. We really don't know it all.

—*Nicholas Kennicott*

Growing up in the Pacific Northwest will give you an irrational love for at least three local institutions: big salmon, dark coffee, and the Seattle Mariners. I fondly remember traveling with my family to see our team in action, even when they were the perennial laughingstock of baseball for their lackluster performance. If you were a Mariners fan in the 1990s, then there is one player who stands head and shoulders in your memories above all others. Ken Griffey Jr. may have been on one of the worst teams around, but he was undisputedly the best player in baseball, and he was ours. Drafted first overall in 1987, Griffey broke into the major leagues at the amazing age of just 19 and quickly earned a very appropriate nickname: The Kid.

We're always amazed by a youngster who can keep up with the grown-ups. This is true not just in sports but also in other areas of life, be they professional, recreational, or even within the church. The health of a local church is too often myopically defined by the presence of a vibrant and growing youth ministry, and evangelicalism seems to always be stocked with a fresh supply of boy-wonder pastors ready to turn the world upside down. If that's the wisdom of our culture, this book is counter-cultural. It's true that being young has its perks, and there is nothing wrong with fresh ideas and youthful energy, but it would be a disaster to become so enamored with youth and its privileges that we neglect the value of age and its wisdom. This book is written by young guys, for young guys, in praise of old guys. It's a plea to our generation to recognize our own limitations and lean on those who have walked these roads before us. They have much to teach us, and we have much to learn.

Although The Kid is still one of my favorite players to don a Mariners cap, the name on the back of my Mariners jersey I wear to games isn't Ken Griffey Jr. It's Jamie Moyer, who on April 17, 2012 became the oldest pitcher to ever record a win in Major League Baseball. During that season he played the game with over 200 other major leaguers who hadn't been born yet when he made his rookie debut in 1986. That's just one more illustration that we young guys underestimate and ignore the old guys at our own expense, and to our own peril.

It is my prayer that this book is both an enjoyable read and a help to many. May the Lord use it for his glory and the blessing of his people.

—*Nicolas Alford*

1

TALKING 'BOUT MY GENERATION

THIS REVOLUTION SHOULD NOT BE TELEVISED

"IT TAKES CONSIDERABLE KNOWLEDGE
JUST TO REALIZE THE EXTENT OF YOUR OWN IGNORANCE."
—THOMAS SOWELL

"EVEN YOUTHS SHALL FAINT AND BE WEARY,
AND YOUNG MEN SHALL FALL EXHAUSTED…"
—ISAIAH 40:30

We're not old guys. Older than some, but not old by our cultural standards. Old enough to have embarked on most of life's major endeavors, but still collecting stones rather than erecting our Ebenezer. Old enough to recognize that our culture places a premium on youth, and to realize the premium can be a dangerous thing.

One of the strangest attributes of modern Christianity is our obsession with the latest thing. Whether it's the most recent game-changer book, the current craze of children's evangelitainment, or this year's freshly minted preacher boy with the cute haircut; in Christendom, fads apparently spring eternal. Let's face it: most of what is marketed to Christians in the modern global West is as disposable as the shifting tastes of the world around us. We say *marketed* on purpose; today's trends in Christianity aren't typically determined through biblical reflection and prayer, they are brainstormed by Madison Avenue-style salesmen and tested out in focus groups long before they ever hit the Evangelical street. That a people called to stand firm upon unchanging truth would be so susceptible to faddish flavor-of-the-month consumerism is both tragic and alarming; the fact that we're often part of the problem is downright convicting.

One fad that passed through evangelicalism some years back was the *life-verse*. A life-verse was exactly what it sounded like: Christians would select a single verse and make it a sort of motto for their life, a maxim they returned to again and again, often inscribing it in their Bible or printing it out, framing it, and hanging it over the kitchen table. So far as fads go, this one was pretty harmless, and difficult to criticize. True, we are called in 2 Timothy 3:16 to make use of *all Scripture*, and the ways that life-verses were often taken out of context could make a hermeneutics professor shed a thousand tears, but who can really stir up the heart to criticize Christians for loving a Bible verse? Even we're not that critical, and that's saying something.

Someone once said that if we were going to hang a Bible verse on our wall, we'd do well to hang it on context wallpaper. That context wallpaper would simply be the surrounding verses of the biblical passage. Doing so would keep us from missing the actual meaning of our life-verse. Case in point: "They who wait for the Lord shall renew their strength; they shall mount up with wings like eagles" (Isaiah 40:31). That's a beautiful statement about how the Lord will sustain and redeem his faithful people, and so it is not surprising that it is a favorite life-verse of many. However, we often read it as a sort of sanctified version of Queen's stadium anthem, *We Are the Champions*. It isn't.

Less well known is the verse immediately preceding it, the one that sets the stage for understanding the necessity of God's promise in verse 31. Isaiah 40:30 reads, "Even youths shall faint and be weary, and young men shall fall exhausted." The reason Scripture utilizes *youths* as an illustration of man's dependence upon God is because youths have the sort of energy and enthusiasm that can carry them further. However, God says that even the young shall faint, grow weary, and fall exhausted without his sustaining grace. Certainly, youthfulness has its perks; but there is also a subtle warning for those who are paying attention: take care lest your youthful vigor carry you further than wisdom warrants. In other words, don't set out on the first five miles of a marathon, only to realize that you haven't actually grown into the shoes on your feet. You don't want those blisters.

Our society is youth-obsessed. Even worse, youth has been idealized to a ludicrous degree. Every spring on the campuses of a thousand colleges and universities, a so-called seasoned veteran of life's trenches takes to the graduation day podium and perpetuates this notion, telling an earnest sea of soft-handed idealists that they are indeed the future and hope of us all. Parents cry, caps are tossed, and celebration ensues in all the wide-eyed and unwrinkled glory that is youth and youthfulness. There is no virtue so unassailable as untried potential.

For many college graduates though, the fun quickly halts when the student loan bills come rolling in and the reality of their situation hits home: *I've thought all along that I'm entitled to a satisfying job with a six-figure salary, but I can't even get hired in an entry-level position.* Numerous sociologists have pointed out that the current up-and-coming generation, *Millennials,* suffers from the most deeply entrenched delusion of entitlement and narcissism the world has ever seen. We're not pointing fingers as if we've found the magic escape hatch, but fully admitting that whether we want to or not, we've believed elements of what American children have been told since the 70's: "You're good enough, you're strong enough, and people like you!"[1] We were horrible at baseball and basketball, but our parent's attics are still full of trophies. We won prizes just for showing up. Our self-esteem was like a fragile flower, carefully guarded at all times. Copernicus was labeled a heretic for saying the earth wasn't the center of the universe, but the new heresy is apparently any suspicion that the universe doesn't revolve around you (and *you* and *you* and *you* and…?). Life was a living Rorschach inkblot test: *What do you see and how does it make you feeeeel?* We're a generation that has been taught that we get to decide life's meaning, and we actually believe it.

---

[1] Adapted from the immortal Stuart Smalley character on *Saturday Night Live.*

In their fascinating book *The Narcissism Epidemic: Living in the Age of Entitlement*, authors Jean Twenge and W. Keith Campbell (both university professors) cite some interesting statistics regarding today's college students. "A survey of college students published in 2008 confirmed [college professor] perceptions. Two-thirds of students believed their professor should give them special consideration if they explained they were trying hard (apparently missing the point that grades are given for performance, not just for trying). One-third believed they deserved at least a B just for attending class. And—perhaps most incredible—one-third thought they should be able to reschedule their final exam if it interfered with their vacation plans."[2] The bottom line is that we've all been taught a destructive idea that couldn't be supported in practice. Namely, that just because we are who we are, the world owes us something. "You can do whatever you want if you try hard and set your mind to it," "Everyone gets a trophy for trying," and "As long as you have fun, that's all

---

[2] Jean M. Twenge and W Keith Campbell, *The Narcissism Epidemic: Living in the Age of Entitlement* (New York: Free Press, 2009), 232.

that matters." Very little time is given to discussions regarding competency or giftedness. If you possess any special skill set, it's just a result of your privilege. If it wasn't, what would it say about all the other boys and girls? That they aren't as skilled? Cover their ears and shut your mouth! How people *feel* is more important than what is *true*. In other words, reality is irrelevant.

We are convinced that the self-esteem driven environment that today's 20 and 30-somethings have been raised in has so alienated many of us from reality that the Church has been deeply impacted. How many young men today are moving from high school graduation, to Bible college, to seminary, and with a master's degree in hand, assume they are automatically entitled to a senior pastor position in a prominent church? Or, convinced that the old paths are outdated and the church is in need of a face-lift, they plant a new church in Awesomeville, the growing metropolis near their hometown.

Don't mistake what we're saying: it's not inherently wrong for a new seminary graduate to land a senior pastor position or for a young man to be a church planter. Being zealous for the work of ministry is not only a good and helpful thing, it's one of the requirements for a man to be an overseer (1 Timothy 3:1). There's something exciting and contagious about a young man who has not been jaded by years of difficult ministry, wanting to charge the gates of hell with a water pistol. We like established local churches, in which each of us serves, and we love church planting. But how many young men do you know who are leaving seminary, not to be senior pastors or church planters, but to take an internship or find an older, wiser man who can shepherd them through the process of becoming an under-shepherd in God's kingdom? It's a countercultural path to take; however, we are convinced it's the best path.

There is a colossal problem in the church today with the self-perceptions and unrealistic expectations of young men in ministry. While it's not axiomatic, it is instructive to note that the Bible often treats age with great reverence (i.e. Psalm 92:12-15) and treats youth as, well... something far less than that (Proverbs 7:7 and the surrounding context are illuminating). As youngish men, we are speaking as insiders. We have been part of the problem, and now we want to propose a solution. So to our generation, we hate to jam a stick into your bicycle spokes and make you fall and rip those trendy jeans, but if you are a young man in pursuit of a life in ministry, the odds that you are much more foolish than you think just went through the roof.

Your youth is perilous. If you show some gifting or potential, especially for ministry, people around you will tend to exaggerate and inflate your true abilities. You will be told you are a better preacher than you actually are. You will be told that you have a better grasp of theology than you actually do. Your fans (we use that word deliberately) will be quick to point to 1 Timothy 4:12 and encourage you to let no one despise your youth (more on this later). A fawning dose of positive feedback may offer an obligatory caution about pride, but the real message will get through because it's the message you've heard your entire life: *you are a very bright young man and everyone is soooo impressed with you.* The poisonous seed is planted, and what quickly springs up is an arrogant attitude that looks down, not on youth, but too often on elders with impatience and scorn. Brothers, let us never forget that we worship the God who sends bears to maul young people who mock the baldness of their elders (2 Kings 2:23-24). That short account from the life of Elisha may befuddle us in many respects, but at the very least we can see in God's eye there's something important about respecting those with alopecia.

What if our generation took a break from trying to speak truth to power and tried listening instead? What would this mean for you? For the church? What would Christ do with a humble army of disciples, quick to listen and slow to speak? Can we even see past the mountainous blind spots of youthful idealism to glimpse such a reality? Remember, our God uses surprisingly simple means to remove mountains. Faith is enough, even to cast mountains into the sea. Our prayer is that God would use this book to cast down the mountains of the youth-enamored-evangelical-complex, and deliver you to smoother paths. So come with us, as we give the old guys their proper due.

2

AGE IS MORE THAN A NUMBER

A THEOLOGY OF WISDOM, EXPERIENCE, AND GRAY HAIR

"THE YEARS TEACH MUCH WHICH THE DAYS NEVER KNEW."
—RALPH WALDO EMERSON

"GRAY HAIR IS A CROWN OF GLORY; IT IS GAINED IN A
RIGHTEOUS LIFE."
—PROVERBS 16:31

In 2015, Americans spent over $114 billion on anti-aging creams, serums, and potions that can be rubbed, smeared, and injected. An additional $113 million is spent by men just to cover up their gray hairs. And while it's likely that the numbers are a bit lopsided because of the existence of Hollywood, each year is filled with nearly 6 million Botox injections. However, the pursuit of everlasting youthfulness didn't begin in Beverly Hills. Vanity isn't the new kid on the block. The Greek Historian Herodotus wrote about a special fountain in the land of the Macrobians that contained water that smelled like violets and was the reported reason the Macrobians were "so long-lived."[3] The famed 16th century conquistador Juan Ponce de Leòn supposedly happened upon the state of Florida in search of the Fountain of Youth. Apparently he didn't find it; he's dead!

There's no doubt that gray hair is a sign of decay that comes as a result of the fall of mankind. People want to stay young, even if they don't understand the deep theology behind that desire. But while the effects of aging may suggest one's proximity to the end of life, they don't suggest immaturity and foolishness. No doubt about it, there are indeed gray-haired fools (Psalm 14:1). The world is not short on people who have rejected their Creator and have sought to live by their own finite wisdom instead of the infinite wisdom of God. But the gray-haired Christian walks around with an advertisement on his head. His silver hat tells everyone that he has been through life's revolving stages, trials and blessings, and has probably picked up a thing or two along the way. Contrary to the world's

---

[3] Herodotus, Book III:23.

annoyance with the elderly, Proverbs 16:31 says that, "Gray hair is a crown of glory; it is gained in a righteous life." A believer with gray hair has a banner signaling you to ask them for advice, counsel, and encouragement. For those silver foxes that have been found enduring in righteousness, their honor is their age, and that age commands your respect. They have a lifetime of education in fighting the same temptations that surround us, engaging in the battle against the world, the flesh, and the devil. An ancient Ugaritic text says, "The greyness of your beard does indeed make you wise."[4] Why would we not take advantage of wisdom that sits in our church every Sunday morning? The decay on the outside is inevitable, but it can be a sure sign of an ever-renewing work of Christ on the inside.

Thomas Brooks writes of the elderly saint:

> Oh! The experiences that he hath of the ways of God, of the workings of God, of the word of God, of the love of God!... Oh! The divine stories that old Christians can tell of the power of the word, of the sweetness of the word, of the usefulness of

---

[4] N. Wyatt, *Religious Texts from Ugarit*, 2nd ed., Biblical Seminar, 53 (London; New York: Sheffield Academic Press, 2002), 101.

the word!… Oh! The stories that he can tell you concerning the love of Christ, the blood of Christ, the offices of Christ, the merits of Christ, the righteousness of Christ, the graces of Christ, and the influence of Christ! Oh! The stories that an old disciple can tell you of the in dwellings of the Spirit, of the operations of the Spirit, of the teachings of the Spirit, of the leadings of the Spirit, of the sealings of the Spirit, of the witnessings of the Spirit, and of the comforts and joys of the Spirit! Oh! The stories that an old Christian can tell you of the evil of sin, the bitterness of sin, the deceitfulness of sin, the prevalence of sin, and the happiness of conquest over sin! Oh! The stories that he can tell you of the snares of Satan, the devices of Satan, the temptations of Satan, the rage of Satan, the malice of Satan, the watchfulness of Satan, and the ways of triumphing over Satan! As an old soldier can tell you of many battles, many scars, many wounds, many losses,

and many victories, even to admiration; so
an old saint is able to tell you many divine
stories even to admiration.[5]

A lifetime of wisdom and an aging body both demand
honor: "You shall stand up before the gray head and honor
the face of an old man, and you shall fear your God: I am
the Lord" (Leviticus 19:32). A person's gray hair means that
we should not only have respect for their knowledge and
experience, but also care for their aging bodies, standing to
give them our chair, our arm, and bearing with them in all
the frustrations that old age brings. It's not easy coming to
terms with the fact that doctor's appointments are more
regular, previously enjoyed activities are less frequent and
more difficult, and driving a car will soon become a thing of
the past. The temptation to boast in his strength is an ever-
present reality in the life of a young man; however, an elderly
saint need not prove himself through physical feats and
games of one-upmanship. He has the snow on top to prove
his worth (Proverbs 20:29).

---

[5] Thomas Brooks, *The Complete Works of Thomas Brooks*, vol. 1
(Edinburgh: James Nisbet &, 1666), 193.

Our culture idolizes youth, but Scripture venerates mature believers. Can you be mature without gray hair? Yes, but the reality is that maturity and wisdom take time. Even the most wise and mature among the youthful still have a lot to learn. No schoolhouse instruction, collection of books, or memorization of facts will be an acceptable substitute for time—time walking with God. "A young carpenter gives more blows and makes more chips, but an old artist doth the most and best work. A young Christian may make most noise in religious duties, but an old Christian makes the best work. A young musician may play more quick and nimble upon an instrument than an old, but an old musician hath more skill and judgment than a young."[6]

Interestingly enough, Scripture tells us that our glorified Lord has white hair: "The hairs of his head were white, like white wool, like snow" (Revelation 1:14a). Perhaps our new, heavenly bodies will include heads that match our robes. They would be crowns worthy of our high calling, those fully conformed to the image of God in Christ.

Faithful local church ministry ought to include specific care for the aged. The quiet old ladies and hard-of-hearing

[6] Ibid.

men are often ignored, but at great loss; the church needs them far more than a new youth pastor with skinny jeans and a soul patch. While the latest parenting trends are being batted around, or those celebrating their 10-year anniversary are giving advice to those who are about to get married, we'd be better served by asking questions and listening to those who have great-grandchildren and have held the same hand in marital bliss through 50 winters. Theologically sound, biblical answers to questions about life are one thing. Theologically sound, biblical answers coupled with decades of experiential successes and failures are completely different. They are far better.

Gray hairs eventually fill the head before they fall out altogether, and it's one sure evidence of a Christian's ascent toward glory. Henry Wadsworth Longfellow wrote in *Evangeline:*

> Then there appeared and spread faint streaks of gray o'er her forehead,
> Dawn of another life, that broke o'er her earthly horizon,

As in the eastern sky the first faint streaks

of the morning.[7]

Gray hair is a foreshadowing of the light of glory breaking in on a believer's life. With it comes the Lord's promise, "Even to your old age I am he, and to gray hairs I will carry you" (Isaiah 46:4). Biblical fidelity demands we view age as more than a number, and that we treasure it along with our God who is at once ever new yet eternally ancient.

---

[7] Henry Wadsworth Longfellow, *Evangeline and Other Poems* (New York: Dover, 1995), 54.

3

MORE WHIPS! MORE SCORPIONS!

HOW NOT TO BE A REHOBOAM

"LEADERS ARE TRUSTED WHEN THEIR LIVES ARE IN
ALIGNMENT WITH THEIR CONVICTIONS."
—ALBERT MOHLER

"A FOOL'S LIPS WALK INTO A FIGHT, AND HIS MOUTH INVITES
A BEATING."
—PROVERBS 18:6

God's Word is not shy with examples of youthful folly. 2 Chronicles 10 is a particularly glaring example, so let's spend some time looking at the chapter. Go read it. Seriously. We'll still be here when you're done.[8]

Our paraphrase of this text renders it simply: dumb young guy takes throne, ignores wise old guys, listens to

---

[8] See also the parallel passage of 1 Kings 12:1-15.

other dumb young guys, one man stoned to death, a nation plunged into rebellion, and a dynasty goes down the tubes (yet even in this the Lord was accomplishing his purposes).

Rehoboam fell for the old premium on youth. As is typical with inexperienced leadership, the empty speech of flattering foolishness won out over the sound counsel of seasoned faithfulness. As it is so very relevant to the subject at hand, let's analyze this episode in some detail.

Rehoboam's most significant deficiency was that "he did not set his heart to seek the LORD" (2 Chronicles 12:14). Surely, no young man who desires to live a life of faithful ministry wants this to be the one-sentence summary of his life. Everything Rehoboam did was shaped by his lack of communion with God, so it's no surprise that when it came to seeking counsel from others, he settled on the guidance of young fools instead of seasoned sages.

Let's look at four elements of youthful folly in this passage, especially as they bear upon local church leadership.

AN AUTOMATIC COMPULSION TO DEPART FROM OLD PATHS

In verse six, King Rehoboam takes counsel with the "old men." The narrator even informs us that these were the very men who served Rehoboam's father Solomon (a guy with a pretty solid reputation for wisdom—he did write most of the Proverbs, after all). Yet in verse eight, he abandons their wise counsel and listens instead to his own inner-circle made up of other young men.

It's very strange that men in Christian ministry, a vocation founded upon the unchanging truth of the gospel, would be so enamored with innovation. We are like salmon distracted by shiny lures; meanwhile our mission never changes: moving against the world current. If truth is truly true, it is incapable of update. What that means is that we must be people of the "old paths" (Jeremiah 6:16). While tradition can be exalted over truth, and a good pedigree is no pardon for falsehood, there should be an obvious preference given to the tested roads others have walked before us. We don't like to think of being "stuck in a rut" as a positive thing, but if a rut has been cut in a faithful path through the long-term testing of years, "stuck in a rut" may be the best place to be.

A FALSE EXALTATION OF FLATTERING FRIENDS

A generation is often an echo chamber unto itself. The men that Rehoboam ends up listening to are those who "had grown up with him" (2 Chronicles 10:8). Typically, people who have the shared experience of coming of age in community with one another already see the same issues, react the same ways, and worry over the same concerns. In his youthful friends, Rehoboam doesn't find actual counsel; he merely finds confirmation. Our peers have a tendency to be nothing more than mirrors of our own image. While this can make for great friendships, it can also lead to deadly blind spots. A wise young man will insist on hearing the counsel of those outside his own generation, and will be very, very slow to dismiss the concerns of his elders.

A POISONOUS PASSION FOR PRIDEFUL POWER

The counsel of the young men centers on how Rehoboam can exalt himself above his father Solomon. They care nothing for the people, beyond their usefulness as stepping-stones for power and voices in praise of young guys. Dale Ralph Davis captures the prideful spirit of the sordid episode:[9]

---

[9] In full disclosure, Davis (in our opinion, one of the best OT commentators writing today) counsels against utilizing this episode as an example of seasoned wisdom and youthful folly (p. 127). However, we believe that 1. His counsel has more relevance to formal preaching, and that 2. It can be legitimate to draw inferences and lessons from texts that are not necessarily the primary intent. J. C. Ryle models this method very well in his *Expository Thoughts on the Gospels.*

These younger bucks believe that nothing impresses like intimidation, nothing tames like threatening. So they give Rehoboam a memorable one-liner to use: 'my little one is thicker than my father's waist' (v. 10b). In case that baffled anyone, they furnished an addendum (v11): 'My father imposed a heavy yoke on you, and I will add to your yoke. My father flogged you with whips, but I will flog you with scorpions' (NJPS). That is relatively clear.[10]

Davis briefly interacts with the open question as to the identity of the *little finger.* Suffice it to say, it is astonishingly prideful, possibly vulgar. Isn't that just like the pride of youth–snickering pleasure in thinking we're clever because we can turn a phrase or shock the older generation's sensibilities. What's far more shocking is our immaturity.

Beware of a self-exalting man, especially if he is doing it all with a smirk. He's not edgy; he's an idiot. The scary thing

---

[10] Dale Ralph Davis. *1 Kings, The Wisdom and the Folly* (Christian Focus: Wales, 2007), 127.

is that we can actually gain quite a bit of prominence through the means of the flesh, but all we're doing is building up our own personal tower of Babel. Our self-made towers have a habit of meeting Jericho's end—they come tumbling down in rubbled ruins. The real tragedy is, we build them up with the deceived souls of people. A man caught up in pride's poison may be able to build a crowd, but all he's doing is gathering future casualties for his inevitable fall and condemnation.

A STUBBORN COMMITMENT TO STUPID DECISIONS

Everyone makes mistakes. Wisdom admits it and corrects the situation; pride clutches tightly to the belief that there are no icebergs out tonight while it rides the Titanic to the bottom of the sea. The intensely negative reaction of the people in verses 16-17 should have given Rehoboam pause; instead, he sent in Hadoram, the taskmaster, and the people shared their feelings with gravel instead of grammar. As it turns out, Mr. Whips and Scorpions runs away like Brave Sir Robin in a Monty Python sketch, but without the comic relief. One suspects Rehoboam was no longer bragging about his "little finger" as he fled, watching his kingdom descend into rebellion.

It is tempting to let Matthew Henry have the last word and end our chapter with this:

> God often fulfills the counsels of his own
> wisdom by infatuating men, and giving
> them up to the counsels of their own folly.
> No more needs to be done to ruin men
> than to leave them to themselves, and
> their own pride and passion.[11]

However, we don't want to end the chapter in that manner. As gospel ministers, we take seriously the call to leave our hearers with hope, even in a bluntly worded chapter of a book. You may have seen yourself in this chapter – you may see ugly elements of your own heart in the spirit of Rehoboam. Your pride may be tightening in around your neck, and the condemnation of your own sin may be choking the spirit out of you. Brother, there is hope. Jesus died for prideful pastors just as much as he died for prostitutes and thieves. His blood can cleanse your

---

[11] Matthew Henry, *Matthew Henry's Commentary on the Whole Bible: Complete and Unabridged in One Volume* (Peabody: Hendrickson, 1994), 588.

conscience; it has a marvelous track record. The same gospel that we preach to others reminds us that our God forgives and restores those who go astray; so after assuring others of his grace, don't find yourself with nothing left for your own wounded conscience. Repent, be restored, change your ways, get up, and keep going.

4

DESPICABLE YOUTH

WHY 1 TIMOTHY 4:12 DOESN'T INVALIDATE THIS BOOK

"IF DO RIGHT, NO CAN DEFENSE."
—MR. MIYAGI

"LET NO ONE DESPISE YOU FOR YOUR YOUTH...."
—1 TIMOTHY 4:12 A

As children of the 1980s, it was impossible for us to escape the cinematic shadow of *The Karate Kid*. Not that we wanted to! It has a perfect blend of earnestness and camp, and actually delivers the occasional great line and solid acting performance (believe it or not, Pat Morita was nominated for an Academy Award for his role as Mr. Miyagi). *Wax on, wax off* may have been the most commonly quoted line, but the most iconic element of the film was the crane-kick. The crane-kick is an utterly silly looking one-footed jump-kick that features prominently in the final fight-scene. It's bad form to give away the ending of a movie (even if it is thirty years old), but in the immortal words of Mr. Miyagi: *if do right, no can defense.*

A lot of people assume that 1 Timothy 4:12 destroys the message of this book. After all, Paul commanded Timothy to *let no one despise him for his youth!* Does not this one verse invalidate our entire argument? This verse is used as what philosophers call a defeater argument, a maxim so conclusive that no further argumentation is needed. It is, say young men everywhere, the silver bullet against the kinds of warnings we are sounding in this book. 1 Timothy 4:12 is revered as a crane-kick to the face for which there is no defense. How can we insist that young men need to be mentored and shepherded along by older and more seasoned brothers in a 1 Timothy 4:12 world? Aren't we just despising youth?

Yes, we are despising youth. So should you. Our message in this chapter is that if you don't despise your own youth, others will rightly despise you for it. Did the Apostle Paul really write this verse to be quoted in order to quench any dissent or criticism of an immature man? Let's look at this verse to find out (hint: he didn't).

THE CRITICAL CONTEXT: *Words From an Old Guy*

This verse is actually an example of everything we are arguing for, so watch out because, well, it's a crane kick alright, and if you're not careful you will kick yourself in the face. The verse is literally an old guy (the Apostle Paul) telling a young guy (Pastor Timothy) how he should conduct himself in ministry. In case you missed the cobra quickness of that statement, here it is again. The primary verse quoted to defend the unassailability of youthful pastors and exalt their fair-haired exuberance is literally a quotation of an old guy speaking truth to a young guy. We would tell our peers that using this verse to push back against input from old guys is the height of irony, but most young guys probably don't actually know what irony is (real irony, not that hipster stuff). Pity.

THE OBVIOUS PRESUPPOSITION: *Your Youth is a Hindrance*

Why does Timothy need this encouragement from Paul? The presupposition is clear: "let no one despise your youth" because people are liable to do exactly that, *despise your youth.* And they're not wrong. In fact, many elements of youth are quite despicable. Immaturity, conceit, and bluster are unbecoming in anyone; in a minister of the gospel they are pure poison.

When Paul gives Timothy this admonition, he is not comprehensively rehabilitating youthfulness from all of its inherent weakness – although you'd think so from the way some quote him! He is calling Timothy to rise above youthful struggles by displaying the sort of wisdom and maturity that is, quite literally, beyond his years. Youth, it seems, is a deficit to be overcome in ministry, not a magic asset.

This is proven when we keep reading verse 12 all the way to the end: *...but set the believers an example in speech, in conduct, in love, in faith, in purity.* Deficiency in those very virtues is commonly associated with youthfulness. Therefore, faithfulness to this command in Scripture never looks like defensively asserting your youth as a virtue in-and-of itself; it looks like rising above the weaknesses of youth through humbly pursuing the sort of belief, speech, conduct, love, faith, and purity that sets an example to the other believers. Your actions must speak louder than your words, or your words will do nothing but loudly announce your immaturity to a watching world.

THE OUTSIDE AUTHORITY: *The Role of the Elders*

There are few things more dangerous to the church than a self-appointed man. One wonders if the young men who wear 1 Timothy 4:12 like an enchanted talisman that exempts them from outside authority have ever kept reading to 1 Timothy 4:14. Just in case you haven't, here's how that goes:

> Let no one despise you for your youth, but set the believers an example in speech, in conduct, in love, in faith, in purity. Until I come, devote yourself to the public reading of Scripture, to exhortation, to teaching. Do not neglect the gift you have, which was given you by prophecy when the council of elders laid their hands on you.[12]

Do you see those last words? Timothy had hands laid on him by the council of elders. This is not an independent man; this is a man under authority. Different denominations may handle this process in slightly different ways, and men may be at diverse stages of ministerial develop-

---

[12] 1 Timothy 4:12-14, ESV.

ment, but that development needs to be happening in the context of a local church with real authority over the man in question. A man who can't find himself in 1 Timothy 4:14 has no right to claim 1 Timothy 4:12.

THE DISCERNIBLE MATURITY: *Don't Be Your Own Hype-Man*

A familiar phenomenon of the hip-hop generation is the hype-man (remember, we're young guys). The job of the hype-man in a hip-hop concert is to get the crowd worked up into frenzy for the emcee who will be actually doing the rapping. The most famous of all hype-men is without question Flavor Flav, the hype-man for Chuck-D and Public Enemy. Even if rap isn't your favored genre, you've probably seen Flav – he's the guy with the giant clock hanging around his neck.

Here's why we're talking about this: hype-men in rap music show more restraint than some young guys in ministry, and at least they're hyping someone else! The pride of some young pastors would be amusing if it wasn't so destructive. These young men can tick off all the glowing stats of their congregation at the drop of a hat, and always go there when their methodology, inexperience, or smug attitudes are questioned in the slightest. Sadly, during the writing of this book, a young pastor was fired from a prominent church, and even in his resignation letter, he couldn't resist hyping his stats.

1 Timothy 4:7-8 calls a pastor to care about personal godliness more than personal hype. Do we? Do we truly care more about growth in holiness and communion with the Lord in the quiet and unseen times of the day than we do about cultivating and maintaining a public platform and popular persona? In verse 15, Paul tells Timothy to "let all see his progress," but he's not talking about increased followers on social media or invitations to speak at conferences. He's talking about the very virtues he just listed out, virtues like purity and love. When a young pastor is progressing in those virtues, he's the opposite of his own hype-man. He knows his own heart too well to plead his own exceptionalism. True godliness always leads you to hype Christ, and Christ alone.

THE CHILLING STAKES: *Crane Kick Counter-Strike*

Mr. Miyagi never said that the crane-kick was indefensible. What he said was *if do **right**, no can defense.* By now we've shown that those who quote 1 Timothy 4:12 like a get-out-of-jail-free card for being young and in ministry aren't doing it right. But before we close this chapter, we need to see how truly harmful it is to get this wrong. In 1 Timothy 4:16, Paul writes: *Keep a close watch on yourself and on the teaching. Persist in this, for by so doing you will save both yourself and your hearers.*

In the context of encouraging Timothy to let no one despise his youth by actively pursuing godly virtue in such a way that he is both an example to others and that his progress is evident to all without saying a word, Paul adds these chilling stakes. The implication is that a man who does not keep close watch on himself and his doctrine is dangerous to himself and others.

The general tone of this book may be pretty light, but this is a deadly serious matter. Brothers, we who have been called into the ministry of the gospel at a young age can be dangerous. The Lord may use us greatly for the edification of his church and the mission of the kingdom, but we can also cause immense harm to the people of God. This is true of a pastor at any age; it is especially true of a young man. Please, if you have been convicted by the message of this book, get help. It's worth it. Don't let your pride be the ruin of God's precious people. Do not take these things lightly.

Do not destroy yourself and your hearers. Brothers, keep a close watch on these things.

If you've been using 1 Timothy 4:12 in all the wrong ways, you need to repent. You need to stop playing pastor and get real. If you don't have older, more mature men who are speaking into your life, you need to get them. True, you might not have elders or even older church members who fit that description in your own congregation. Are there older pastors in your community or denomination that you can rely on for wisdom? There is simply no excuse for an independent young pastor without mentors and counselors. Put down the book, pick up the phone, and call an old guy. (Just as long as it's before 9:00pm; they go to bed early.)

5

LIKE FATHER, LIKE SON

PAUL AND TIMOTHY AS A BETTER WAY

"OLD MAN LOOK AT MY LIFE;
I'M A LOT LIKE YOU WERE."
—NEIL YOUNG

"TO TIMOTHY, MY TRUE CHILD IN THE FAITH."
—1 TIMOTHY 1:2

In the fifth century, the ancient Greek physician Hippocrates penned what is now known as the Hippocratic oath. Even today, the oath is taken by Western medical doctors upon completion of their training and entrance into the world of medicine. While Hippocrates was no Christian, he did understand something of the significance of a mentoring relationship for those who would continue to hone and improve the art and science of medicine in the generations ahead. Part of the oath states:

I swear by Apollo the physician, and Aesculapius the surgeon, likewise Hygeia and Panacea, and call all the gods and goddesses to witness, that I will observe and keep this underwritten oath, to the utmost of my power and judgment. I will reverence my master who taught me the art. Equally with my parents, will I allow him things necessary for his support, and will consider his sons as brothers. I will teach them my art without reward or agreement; and I will impart all my acquirement, instructions, and whatever I know, to my master's children, as to my own; and likewise to all my pupils, who shall bind and tie themselves by a professional oath, but to none else.

Given the cost of medical school these days, we are guessing there have been some crafty interpretations of, "I will teach them my art without reward…" however, the point is well made. Throughout the ancient world, these kinds of mentoring relationships were the primary means of education. Trades and crafts were taught through experiencing them together.

We are very grateful for our educations and thank God for the opportunities we've had to receive formal academic training from some brilliant men of the faith. However, we believe that the greatest education for any young man pursuing a life of pastoral ministry isn't in a classroom with a career academic, but in a local church with an older, wiser man who has been a pastor for many years. Often, the most difficult problems we encounter in ministry aren't dealt with in seminary training because they can't be. Many of the trials awaiting us in ministry come down to simply needing experience in the school of hard-knocks.

The Apostle Paul invested in his young pastor protégé, Timothy. Paul called Timothy his "true child in the faith" (1 Timothy 1:2). On Paul's second missionary journey, he met the young man Timothy in Lystra (Acts 16). Timothy's early spiritual formation came through his mother Eunice and grandmother Lois (2 Timothy 1:5). His father was a Greek, so he did not have a Christian man providing a foundational basis for faith in his life. We aren't told what Paul saw in the young man. Perhaps there was an evident giftedness, or simply a compassionate desire on the part of Paul to provide Timothy with the fathering he hadn't received. Whatever the circumstances, Timothy's experience with Paul was a priceless blessing that was of tremendous value for the entire church; it was a relationship worth emulating as the best way forward for young men who are moving into a life of pastoral ministry.

Young pastors who don't have older, wiser pastors to turn to for wisdom, correction, and training are dangerous. They're a potential danger to God's flock, their own family, and their own faith. All of us have blind spots we're totally oblivious to—that's why we call them *blind* spots. So the potential for young men like us to make shipwreck of our responsibilities and ourselves is massive. Young men like Timothy need older men like Paul—wise, seasoned, humble, gracious fathers in the faith helping pave a way forward for those of us who are still full of youth and vigor in the earliest days of our ministries. Paul's desire was to keep Timothy from thinking and acting like he needed to be an obnoxious trailblazer for the church. Paul wanted Timothy to be a model of ministry and a model for other gospel ministers that reflected what he had seen in those of previous generations, and particularly in the Apostle Paul himself. So Paul offers to Timothy his sound wisdom, instructing him to keep his focus on a few main things, especially after Paul was dead and gone.

Paul's two letters to Timothy offer a tremendous amount of insight into the relationship they shared. The first letter is a manual of sorts for how to conduct matters within the church. Elders, deacons, preaching—it's all in there, and if the Evangelical Church would pay closer attention to what Paul has written in this one letter, many of the ills that plague us in these days would be healed.

Paul's second letter to Timothy is his final correspondence, calling him to continued faithfulness to the King and his kingdom. Old Paul wants young Timothy to hold fast to the faith he knows and has been taught, by the power of the Holy Spirit, not wavering from what Paul has entrusted to him. 2 Timothy is a very personal letter, filled with love and affection for Timothy. It's the Apostle's last will and testament, written just prior to his death. Another old man, John Calvin, said the letter was "written not with ink but with Paul's own blood."[13]

---

[13] John Calvin and William Pringle, *Commentaries on the Epistles to Timothy, Titus, and Philemon* (Bellingham, WA: Logos Bible Software, 2010), 179.

When Paul writes to Timothy, his pastoral insight differs significantly from what is often provided in today's pragmatic culture. Paul never comes close to suggesting that his eyes should be set on Christianizing and incorporating the latest fads into the worship and practice of the church, or that he should consult the leadership gurus of his day to find insights into how to grow ye olde Church of Ephesus into a mega church called *The Well*, *The Porch*, *The Aura*, or whatever other trendy name seems cool that year. On the contrary, Paul tells Timothy, "I am writing these things to you so that... you may know how one ought to behave in the household of God, which is the church of the living God, a pillar and buttress of the truth" (1 Timothy 3:14-15). While young men are full of creative, innovative ideas about how to grow local churches and keep people engaged, Paul indicates certain things that must be present in any faithful, God-honoring ministry.

When the Apostle writes in 1 Timothy 3:15 that the church is the "pillar and buttress of the truth" he is saying that the church is the foundation and column upon which the truth of God stands. The truth Paul means is, "the mystery of godliness" (1 Timothy 3:16). It's right to conclude that the truth of God's Word has been entrusted to the Church, and the Church has been given the responsibility of preserving and communicating that received truth so the people of God might worship God as God and have everlasting communion with Him. In other words, God is not calling his people to reinvent the wheel that has already been rolling for the last 2,000 years.

The Bible, and especially the Apostle Paul in his letters to Timothy, indicates that the church holds a deposit, a pattern—a tradition!—and has a responsibility to pass these down from one generation to the next. In a self-obsessed world of pop-culture, the Church is called to build upon a foundation that has already been laid, not one dreamed up in a vision-casting brainstorm session around soy lattes and kale chips.

DEPOSIT

Paul uses a legal term describing something placed in another person's trust for safekeeping. The term is used here to focus on something that is passed on from elder to elder, from church to church, from one generation to the next. The deposit being made is part of what Jesus had in mind when he gave his final instructions to the disciples saying, "Go therefore and make disciples of all nations, baptizing them in the name of the Father and of the Son and of the Holy Spirit, *teaching them to observe all that I have commanded you*" (Matthew 28:19-20, emphasis added). The deposit is the teaching of God; it is the gospel and all its inherent doctrines.

Paul writes, "O Timothy, guard the deposit entrusted to you. Avoid the irreverent babble and contradictions of what is falsely called 'knowledge,' for by professing it some have swerved from the faith" (1 Timothy 6:20). Paul himself was given a deposit (2 Timothy 1:12), which he then gave to Timothy, instructing the young pastor, "By the Holy Spirit who dwells within us, guard the good deposit entrusted to you" (2 Timothy 1:14). The Apostle's concern is that Timothy understands and passes on that which has been entrusted to him instead of building a new foundation. He tells Timothy, "Keep a close watch on yourself and on the teaching [i.e. The deposit that has been entrusted to you]," (1 Timothy 4:16).

PATTERN

The Lord presented a pattern through Paul's life and words that was worthy of emulation. "Follow the pattern of the sound words that you have heard from me, in the faith and love that are in Christ Jesus" (2 Timothy 1:13). The Apostle never backs down from calling the young pastor to do as he does, to teach as he teaches, and to live as he lives. This is the role of a faithful mentor: establish a pattern worth emulating, and call men to follow it. Paul tells Timothy, "But as for you, continue in what you have learned and have firmly believed, knowing from whom you learned it" (2 Timothy 3:14).

A faithful pastor is one who "must hold firm to the trustworthy word as taught, so that he may be able to give instruction in sound doctrine and also to rebuke those who contradict it" (Titus 1:9). Young men ought to see this modeled by older men first, lest they walk into a disastrous situation they are ill prepared for. Follow the pattern, not your instinct or your own ideas.

TRADITION

We are not talking about the traditions of man, but the traditions of God. Tradition is a positive synonym for the teaching of Christ and the Apostles. In fact, the Apostle Paul instructs the church at Thessalonica that they are able to determine whether or not someone is walking in the faith by whether or not they adhere to the tradition that was received from the Apostles (2 Thessalonians 3:6). Implied in the word tradition is a focus on that which has already been established, not something new, flashy, or trendy.

CONCLUSION

Jesus says in Luke 6:40, "A disciple is not above his teacher, but everyone when he is fully trained will be like his teacher." The truth is, every man will learn from someone or something. Nobody thinks and plans in a vacuum. So who is it that we want to be like? A young minister of the gospel ought to find a man who, like the Apostle Paul, can hand over the deposit, lay down the pattern, and adhere to the tradition that has been established in the Bible. We ought to be humble men who, like Timothy, will take the instruction of our mentors and follow their example. In the end, Paul commends Timothy for his leadership in the church and how he did what we are hoping you will do also: "You, however, have followed my teaching, my conduct, my aim in life, my faith, my patience, my love, my steadfastness" (2 Timothy 3:10).

There are plenty of trailblazers in modern evangelicalism, and the Bible doesn't speak too highly of them. They've disregarded the wisdom of our fathers and have sought to go their own way in hopes of being fawningly admired and wielding great influence. However, Proverbs 15:5 tells us, "A fool despises his father's instruction, but whoever heeds reproof is prudent." Don't be a hero. We already have one in Jesus, and he doesn't need any sidekicks. Be humble, serve faithfully, and listen to the instruction of the men who have gone before us. They know far more than we realize.

6

IN PRAISE OF *REALLY* OLD GUYS

WHY DEAD THEOLOGIANS ARE THE LIFE OF THE PARTY

"GIVE YOURSELF UNTO READING. THE MAN WHO NEVER READS WILL NEVER BE READ; HE WHO NEVER QUOTES WILL NEVER BE QUOTED. HE WHO WILL NOT USE THE THOUGHTS OF OTHER MEN'S BRAINS, PROVES THAT HE HAS NO BRAINS OF HIS OWN. YOU NEED TO READ."
—CHARLES HADDON SPURGEON

"THEREFORE, SINCE WE ARE SURROUNDED BY SO GREAT A CLOUD OF WITNESSES, LET US ALSO LAY ASIDE EVERY WEIGHT, AND SIN WHICH CLINGS SO CLOSELY, AND LET US RUN WITH ENDURANCE THE RACE THAT IS SET BEFORE US, LOOKING TO JESUS, THE FOUNDER AND PERFECTER OF OUR FAITH."
—HEBREWS 12:1-2

C.S. Lewis once wrote an introduction to *De Incarnatione Verbi Dei*, which was the work of Athanasius, the fourth-century bishop of Alexandria, on the incarnation of Christ. In his introduction, Lewis actually has very little to say directly about Athanasius and his work, but instead provides a treatise on the importance of reading works of antiquity that have survived the ages. Lewis' wisdom is practical and sound: "It is a good rule, after reading a new book, never to allow yourself another new one till you have read an old one in between. If that is too much for you, you should at least read one old one to every three new ones."

In the digital age, Lewis' exhortation increases in importance. Whether it's a blessing or a curse is yet to be known in its entirety, but with eReaders, instant downloads, self-publishing, blogs, and social media, the constant temptation is to keep up with the new, leaving very little time for the old. There's also an incredible blessing that comes with the digital age—the ability to reprint older works that were previously left to dusty bookshelves, and even to digitize and make them searchable on a variety of platforms. But printed words are only useful if we read them, and anything worth studying is likely to populate more space than 140 characters. It's no secret that most young people in the 21st Century have an attention span commensurate with a hummingbird, so to pick up and read an old book, even with a new flashy cover, is an unlikely endeavor for most. It just *sounds* like a difficult task to read something by someone 450 years your senior with all that old language and lack of youthful flair. Different times; different customs; different lives. We wouldn't want to commit the mortal sin of appearing to be irrelevant.

Snark aside, the greatest reluctance to read the dead guys is a misconception that it takes reading five other books to understand the one in front of me. However, reading far into the past is not as difficult as most assume. Lewis explains:

> There is a strange idea abroad that in every subject the ancient books should be read only by the professionals, and that the amateur should content himself with the modern books. Thus I have found as a tutor in English Literature that if the average student wants to find out something about Platonism, the very last thing he thinks of

doing is to take a translation of Plato off the library shelf and read the Symposium. He would rather read some dreary modern book ten times as long, all about "isms" and influences and only once in twelve pages telling him what Plato actually said. The error is rather an amiable one, for it springs from humility. The student is half afraid to meet one of the great philosophers face to face. He feels himself inadequate and thinks he will not understand him. But if he only knew, the great man, just because of his greatness, is much more intelligible than his modern commentator. The simplest student will be able to understand, if not all, yet a very great deal of what Plato said; but hardly anyone can understand some modern books on Platonism. It has always therefore been one of my main endeavours as a teacher to persuade the young that firsthand knowledge is not only more worth acquiring than secondhand

knowledge, but is usually much easier and
more delightful to acquire.

It's difficult to imagine many more important questions
when considering a person's leadership potential than,
"What have you read that has been most influential in your
life?" And herein lies an important warning: If every work a
man mentions has been written and published within the
last ten years, his well of wisdom to draw from will be
shallow, and he will likely be consumed by the latest
methods and fads. Surely in the Church, a man who is being
considered for the role of a pastor-theologian must be
shaped and guided by the Bible, but let's not be simplistic.
Even cult leaders say Scripture leads them. Most men who
are pursuing God's call into ministry have spent time in a
seminary classroom and a theological library reading a
relatively small collection of the important works of their
tradition, and rightfully so. The educational process for
anyone who leads, preaches, teaches, or wants to be a
productive member of society is ongoing. If you paid
attention in school, hopefully you've read some good works
because you *had* to, but the truly wise are those who have
continued to read good works because they *want* to; indeed
they have a deep sense that they *must*.

It would be wrong for any church to expect a man to have mastered all the great works of the Western tradition, to be able to give in-depth exposition of all the historic creeds and confessions, or to have done a comparative analysis of antidisestablishmentarianism's influence among 17th Century dissenters and those who led the American revolution, before they're ready to serve as a pastor. However, the Bible's qualifying mark of a man being "able to teach" (1 Timothy 3:2) implies that he possesses more than a rudimentary knowledge of the Scriptures which must include his having worked with the ideas of others. A man cannot possibly read everything of value, but he should always be reading something, and in time his convictions will change, his horizons will expand, and his ability to engage ideas and lead others will improve. We contend that the surest paths to these ends are the old paths—well worn, trusted, and not susceptible to change. The dead guys and their writings that we love today won't have to be questioned in the future because of a theological or moral nose-dive after years of faithful ministry. The benefit of a man being dead is that we can know the entirety of his life instead of waiting to see what will come of it. This is not to imply that old equals good and new equals bad, lest we discredit our own work in the book you're reading right now; everything was new at some point (although the content of our book is, we hope, very old). But there's great value in that which has been tried, trusted, and found to be true. There are few tests of greater value than time.

We realize we haven't done much so far to answer the looming question: What dead guys should we hang out with? Depending on the desired end, the answer to this question can vary greatly, however there are some broad categories to help direct our steps.

CLASSICAL LITERATURE

In the classical tradition, there is continual reference to the *Great Conversation*. Philosophers and poets have been locked in the volley of ideas since the beginning of time. The conversation is unavoidable, but most westerners are ignorant to the fact that it's even going on. Over the last decade there has been a recovery of classical education and the reading of what has long been known as the Great Books. Whether we know what those books say or not, they have been the most instrumental ideas in shaping the development of human societies from age-to-age. Any man who thinks the writings of Aristotle, Hesiod, Augustine, or

Dostoevsky are irrelevant today has much to learn, and would do well to avoid positions of leadership lest he cause a host of others to walk in error with him.

The great books are called great for a reason. The intention is not to suggest that the reader will necessarily like or agree with what they've read (in fact, if you agree with *some* of the classical works, we'd be very concerned about your sanity and the safety of your neighbors). However, the ideas of the great books have been compelling enough to shape culture, for good or evil.

Christians, and especially those who are interested in leadership within the Church, should interact with what was once read in any standard Western education. For example, whose ideas of paradise do you find more compelling, Dante or Milton? Which playwright presents a more realistic picture of life and human nature, Aristophanes or Shakespeare? Who would you rather have as the primary advisor to your nation's top leader, Plato or Thucydides? A foray into the classics will dramatically change how one looks at the world around them; it will alter the way one thinks and reasons through arguments, reads the Bible, looks at the role of government, and assess whether change is always for the better. Join the Conversation!

If you have the intellectual capacity to exposit and teach the Word of God, you possess the requisite tools to understand the classics. As Mr. Lewis suggested earlier, it's probably not as difficult as you might think. One word of caution while participating in the Great Conversation: As with all other conversations, it's important to start at the beginning. If you jump into the middle, there's a high likelihood that you will be frustrated with a misunderstanding of references and allusion to previous works. The writers of the great books assume their readers have already read what others have written.[14]

PATRISTICS

The Church fathers (*Patristics*) provide a fascinating look into the earliest available literature regarding Christian theology and practice, other than the Bible itself. The Patristic writings cover the time period of approximately the end of the Apostolic Period (c. 100 AD) through the beginning of the Medieval Period (c. 600 AD) of Church

---

[14] See Bibliography.

history. In many respects, the patristics were the trailblazers of the Christian faith in its second generation. Having been so close to the Apostolic Period, the Patristics' theological insights are fascinating (and sometimes bizarre), although not inspired or always accurate.[15] However, their most prominent contributions have been the refutation of early heresies and errors, and the formulation of a robust Christology and Trinitarianism that materialized in the midst of ecclesiastical controversies. Many of the creeds of the Church that are respected and used today were written in the Patristic Period to help clarify the Church's theological identity. Roman Catholicism, Eastern Orthodoxy, and Protestantism all claim at least partial continuity with the Patristics, so reading their primary sources helps us understand each other's claims.

MEDIEVAL THEOLOGY

To many Christians, the Medieval Period is a no-man's land, thought to be so littered with philosophical speculation that any attempt to extract anything of value for protestant, evangelical use is a fool's errand. However, a

---

[15] See, for example, the 1st-2nd Century work *The Shepherd of Hermas*.

discerning reader will learn to eat the meal before them while spitting out the bones. Certainly, some Medieval theologians like Peter Lombard were a formidable mess, but others like Bernard of Clairvaux who wrote *On Loving God*—a heartwarming masterpiece—should be read widely and joyfully by Christians of every age. Anselm's pivitol work *de Homo* should be read by anyone who loves the cross of Christ, and while Gottschalk is known as the miserable monk, he had some wonderful things to say.

Thomas Aquinas has long been referenced in numerous Christian traditions, and is arguably most responsible for adapting the writings of Aristotle for use in the Church. John Wycliffe has been called *The Morning Star of the Reformation.* Nearly 200 years before Martin Luther, Wycliffe fought against the corruptions he saw in the church to include the veneration of saints, the sale of indulgences, the doctrine of transubstantiation, the authority of the pope, and the exaltation of tradition over Scripture. Wycliffe is credited as one of the first men to have set out to translate the Scriptures into the common language of the people.

REFORMATION-ERA THEOLOGY

A lot of young men like to talk about Martin Luther, and may have even read a biography or two about his life and work (there's no shortage of them[16]). After all, Luther is a compelling historical figure, and the stories about him are captivating. A large library of Luther's works are readily available, translated into English, and should be studied as primary sources. There are few men in Church history as important and controversial as Luther, and a read through his writings and sermons is a fascinating journey. Likewise, with the rise of New Calvinism, there is no shortage of young theologians talking about Calvin who have never read his works. Sadly, the efforts of one of the greatest theologians the world has known have been condensed down to five points that he personally did not even formulate. Calvin's commentaries, sermons, and his *magnum opus, The Institutes of the Christian Religion,* are as easy to understand and are as devotionally rich as the hottest new book off the press. The Protestant churches of today owe their existence to these men and their con-

---

[16] We know of a good one.

temporaries, so we would do well to understand them and the riches they've left behind.

PURITAN THEOLOGY

Since the 1950s, the writings of the Puritans have been collected and reprinted in large quantities. Presbyterian, Congregational, and Baptistic Christians can all trace their early roots back to the 16th and 17th Century Puritans who produced an astronomical amount of Christian literature. Today, confessionally reformed Christians are linked to the Puritan-era through the creeds they subscribe to and the resulting practices in the life of the local church. It would be grossly understated to say that the Puritans alone will provide any Christian with a lifetime of reading that will encourage, convict, sharpen, and shape their hearts in a way that makes them love Christ and his people with greater zeal and efficacy. Since the days of the Apostles, the Reformation and Puritan eras have provided the most significant contribution to experiential, biblical and systematic theology. Among the Puritans you will find names like Thomas Brooks, John Bunyan, Jeremiah Burroughs, Stephen Charnock, Matthew Henry, and John Owen. *Meet the Puritans: With a Guide to Modern*

Reprints by Joel Beeke and Randall Pederson[17] is an invaluable resource for beginner and experienced Puritan readers alike.

OTHER IMPORTANT DEAD GUYS

In our tradition, it's impossible to escape the legacy of the Prince of Preachers, Mr. Charles Haddon Spurgeon. The Spurgeon Archive online claims that, "Today, there is available more material written by Spurgeon than by any other Christian author, living or dead."[18] Spurgeon's books and sermons are among the most readable of all Christian literature, and we suggest using his works in preparation for your own sermons and Bible studies, as well as enjoying them devotionally. Young men should especially take the time to work through the 4 volumes of *Lectures to my Students* and the book *An All-Round Ministry*. We would also recommend becoming familiar with Spurgeon's life and ministry through various biographical works including *The*

---

[17] Beeke, Joel R., and Randall J. Pederson, *Meet the Puritans: With a Guide to Modern Reprints* (Grand Rapids: Reformation Heritage Books, 2006).

[18] Eric Hayden, "Did You Know?," The Spurgeon Archive, accessed May 5, 2014, http://www.spurgeon.org/spurgn2.htm.

Forgotten Spurgeon by Iain Murray, *Living By Revealed Truth: The Life and Pastoral Theology of Charles Haddon Spurgeon* by Tom Nettles, and *Spurgeon: A New Biography* by Arnold Dallimore. You will be inspired, convicted, and reminded that there will only ever be one C.H. Spurgeon in this world.

Martyn Lloyd-Jones is another important dead guy who provides us with a massive collection of resources. Pertinent to our focus in this book are Lloyd-Jones' *Authority* and his oft-cited work *Preaching and Preachers*. Lloyd-Jones is often remembered by his Friday evening lectures through the Apostle Paul's letter to the Romans, and his 232 sermons on Paul's letter to the Ephesians. He was a remarkably gifted expository preacher who gave up a promising future in medicine to pursue a life of faithful pulpit ministry. Lloyd-Jones' sermons were as warm, pastoral, and practical as anything you might hear today. He was a true experiential Calvinist with a fervent evangelistic zeal. You will be greatly encouraged to read *Life of Martyn Lloyd-Jones - 1899-1981* by Iain Murray or watch the documentary *Logic on Fire*. Additionally, the MLJ Trust has made all of Lloyd-Jones' recorded sermons and lectures available for free online.

LETTING DEAD GUYS SPEAK

From reading this chapter you may have gotten the impression that most of our best friends are dead guys. That's true, and it's probably why we never got invited to parties in high school. Yet after spending hours thinking along with J. C. Ryle in his *Expository Thoughts of the Gospel,* or yearning together with Jonathan Edwards for *Heaven: A World of Love,* or interacting with any number of these other dearly departed men, how can they be considered anything other than our precious friends? And even more than friends, they are our teachers, counselors, and mentors. Yes, the discussions can be a bit one-sided, but not in the direction you might think when talking to a dead guy. We've actually found it most beneficial to shut our mouths and let the dead guys carry the conversation.

CONCLUSION

GO WEST YOUNG MAN

WHERE TO GROW FROM HERE

"SPEAKING FIGURATIVELY, THE STUDY OF THEOLOGY OFTEN
PRODUCES OVERGROWN YOUTHS WHOSE INTERNAL ORGANS
HAVE NOT CORRESPONDINGLY DEVELOPED. THIS IS A
CHARACTERISTIC OF ADOLESCENCE. THERE IS ACTUALLY
SOMETHING LIKE THEOLOGICAL PUBERTY."
—HELMUT THIELICKE

"THUS SAYS THE LORD: 'STAND BY THE ROADS, AND LOOK,
AND ASK FOR THE ANCIENT PATHS, WHERE THE GOOD WAY
IS; AND WALK IN IT, AND FIND REST FOR YOUR SOULS...'"
—JEREMIAH 6:16A

We hope by now you're thoroughly convinced of youth's unavoidable shortcomings, and of the inestimable value of the old guys' wisdom. You may, however, be left with a greater sense of conviction than a practical call to action. The purpose of this conclusion is to give you some steps you can take, concrete action to address the glaring shortcomings of a youthful minister.

FIND HELP

The way you start to climb out of a hole is to stop digging. Hopefully, if you're a pastor, there is a network of fellow ministers you are in regular contact with. This network may be through local connections, denominational ties, or even longstanding friendships now maintained over social media. Whatever it looks like for you, it's essential to have a network of brothers to support you in your calling and labors. Assuming you have such a network (if you don't, start cultivating one immediately), take a look at who these men are. Are they mirror reflections of you? Are they similar in age, temperament, and experience? If so, admit to yourself that they're probably also similar to you in weaknesses, blind spots, and immaturity. Even worse, if you're the sole sage of the group, the one that others are always coming to for wisdom and academic brilliance, recognize that you're in a truly precarious place. The most dangerous place in the game is always king of the hill. Hills are made to fall from.

Here's what you need to do: get yourself some old guys. Build a network of older, more experienced men with whom you have regular contact. You may need to chase them a bit, because the best old guys tend to be too humble to see their own value, but thankfully you're probably faster than they are. Youth does actually still have a perk or two. So first, build up a network of older men whose wisdom you seek and whose input you value.

Although this must include experienced gospel ministers, don't discount older men who have lived the Christian life faithfully outside of vocational ministry. There is perspective and wisdom that is essential to hear from men outside of pastoral labors. The people we are called to minister to don't live their lives in a pastor's study; they live in the everyday trenches of secular life. Make sure at least some of the hands guiding you have some dirt of the world under their fingernails.

SEEK MENTORS

After you've connected with some older, more experienced men, seek out at least one formal mentor. Ask them to speak regularly with you about your life, ministry, and any other pertinent issues. Spend time with them. Watch how they treat their wives and families. Ask them for book recommendations. Talk through difficult church issues with them. Resist the urge to teach them the latest views on the theological fad of the day; this is a time for learning.

The best course of action may be to pursue a formal ministry internship. Each church handles this differently, but many older pastors will be very willing to pour into a younger man for a focused number of years. In fact, we would be so bold as to say this is the best step for a young man to take immediately after, or even during seminary studies. True, not all men have that providential opportunity, but if you do, don't turn aside from it lightly.

Even if you're too far down the road of life to take an internship, you never outgrow the call to discipleship. Christianity is discipleship, at its very core (Matthew 28:19, Titus 2). You should always be discipling others, and you should always be being discipled. Don't settle for a casual relationship that soothes your conscience; engage Christ's discipleship call like you really believe the Son of God is the one who told you to do it.

This is a concept with a rich biblical pedigree. In 2 Timothy 2:2 there are actually five distinct parties involved in mentorship. There is the core mentor/mentee relationship of Paul and Timothy. This is happening in the context of "many witnesses," a reference to the local church.

Furthermore, Paul charges Timothy to take up the discipleship baton and entrust it to "faithful men." But even then the discipleship chain reaction isn't finished: those faithful men are to be poured into so that they "will be able to teach others also." Paul's vision for pastoral training is multigenerational mentorship in the context of the local church.

READ WIDELY

Take an inventory of the last ten books you've read (seriously... what are the last ten books you've read?). When were they published? What voices are loudest in your life? What's the dominant worldview you're feeding into your soul? Is it the chronological snobbery of exclusive modernity, or is it a healthy mix of contemporary input with the best voices of the past?

We'd never say that you shouldn't read the best new books. As a pastor, you need to know what's going on in the kingdom and you need to listen in on the ongoing theological conversations of our age. But take C. S. Lewis' words to heart (see chapter six) and consider the ratio of old to new in your current reading selections.

STAY HUMBLE

History is full of men with greater gifts than you who made a wreckage of their lives and ministries because of pride. Pride is a poison that will intoxicate you with the pretended taste of honey. Spit it out. The insanity of sin is always manifest in self-reliance, so whose power are you relying on to fulfill your ministry? Never forget that your heart is more fallen, your motives are more mixed, and your talents are less pronounced than you ever think. Let's be clear: God doesn't need you. Jesus doesn't need you. The Holy Spirit doesn't need you. Men have been pastoring the church for thousands of years, and the kingdom will be in fine shape after you're dead. God always has his workers; even a donkey will do in a pinch.

Does that mean you don't matter? Wonder upon wonders, it actually doesn't. That the God who doesn't need us chooses to not only love and redeem us from our sins, but even to call some into his direct ministry of service is a token to his grace alone. The sooner you mortify the pride of a youthful pastorate the better. Until you do, you are a man unfit for public consumption. There is, as J. C. Ryle has taught, enough remaining sin in you to burn as hot as hell if the Lord gave leave to the first sparks of your wickedness. Brothers, stay humble. The stakes are life and death.

GET OLD

There's no shortcut to this one. Horace Greeley once said concerning the Westward expansion of the American nation, "Washington is not a place to live in. The rent is high, the food is bad, the dust is disgusting and the morals are deplorable. Go West young man, go West and grow up in the county."[19] Without defending the absurdity of Manifest Destiny, there is a spirit to that charge which all young men should readily adopt. It wouldn't be hard to recast it concerning the perils of youth and the call to grow up "to mature manhood, to the measure of the stature of the fullness of Christ" (Ephesians 4:13b). That's the country you want to grow up in, not the echo chamber of your own self-cultivated praise. After all, the food is bad and the morals are deplorable.

If you want to be the old guy in the room that the younger men look to, there is only way to get there: the grace of God. "Who is sufficient for these things?" the

---

[19] Greeley, Horace. *New York Tribune*, July 13, 1865.

Apostle Paul exclaimed when he considered the awesome weight of pastoral ministry (2 Corinthians 2:16). He went on: "For we are not, like so many, peddlers of God's word, but as men of sincerity, as commissioned by God, in the sight of God we speak in Christ" (v. 17).

You live your life; you fulfill your calling; you labor in your ministry before the face of God. Don't settle for peddling when God calls you to preach. Don't bank on your youth when God calls you to invest in long-term faithfulness. You are a man commissioned of God to speak in Christ with sincerity, or you should resign your pastorate tomorrow. But don't quit so quickly. If God has called you, he will give you grace to keep running the race. It's like the old guys love to sing: "Grace has led me safe thus far, and grace will lead me home." By grace, young men like us can one day come to the finish line and say, "I have fought the good fight, I have finished the race, I have kept the faith" (2 Timothy 4:7). The beautiful promise of local church pastoral mentorship is, according to 2 Timothy 2:2, we who are looking for spiritual fathers now are called to invest in the next generation, even to grow into the role of spiritual grandfathers and beyond. This is how Christ builds his church; this is how the gates of hell will never prevail.

No pastor ever became a faithful old guy because he was a talented young guy. He got there by grace alone. By grace alone, you too can be that old guy, but only through the sustaining power of God. The gospel you preach to others is your hope also.

So, as we close this book, let's praise the old guys; but above all else, let's praise the one who is ever old and ever new; always is and ever was; the beginning and the end, Alpha and Omega, and everything in between. To God be the glory, both now and forevermore. Amen.

Appendix:

Suggested Reading

"WHEN I GET A LITTLE MONEY, I BUY BOOKS. IF ANY IS LEFT,
I BUY FOOD AND CLOTHES."
—ERASMUS

"WHEN YOU COME, BRING THE CLOAK THAT I LEFT WITH
CARPUS AT TROAS, ALSO THE BOOKS, AND ABOVE ALL THE
PARCHMENTS."
—1 TIMOTHY 4:13

Each of these books are listed as suggestions from the categories mentioned in chapter six. Some of the works will give you a greater love for God and his work in creation and redemption. Some of the works will leave you with strong disagreements and a reminder of the extreme difference between the kingdom of God and the world. It's important, especially as a young guy, to read widely and read often, and these are some of the most read works throughout history worth your time and effort. There are, of course, many more that could rightfully be added, but this list is a good start.

CLASSICAL LITERATURE

Hesiod, *Theogony, Works and Days*

Virgil, *The Aeneid*

Plato, *The Republic, Apology of Socrates, Symposium, Euthyphro*

Thucydides, *Peloponnesian War*

Aristophanes, *Clouds, Frogs, Peace, Birds*

Aeschylus, *Prometheus*

Sophocles, *The Oedipus Cycle*

Euripides, *The Bacchae, Hippolytus*

Aristotle, *Nichomachean Ethics, Politics, Rhetoric, Poetics*

Machiavelli, *Mandragola, The Prince*

Shakespeare, *Henry V, King Lear, Tempest, Merchant of Venice, Macbeth*

Nietzsche, *Beyond Good and Evil, Genealogy of Morals, Twilight of the Idols*

Dostoyevsky, *The Brothers Karamazov*

EARLY CHURCH/MEDIEVAL THEOLOGY

Aquinas, *Summa Theologica*

Augustine, *City of God, Confessions*

Bernard of Clairveaux, *On the Necessity of Loving God*

Dante, *The Divine Comedy*

REFORMATION-ERA THEOLOGY

Calvin, *The Institutes of the Christian Religion*

The Heidelberg Catechism

Knox, *History of the Reformation in Scotland*

Luther, *95 Theses, The Freedom of the Christian, A Commentary on St. Paul's Epistle to the Galatians, Bondage of the Will*

PURITAN THEOLOGY

Any of the Puritan Paperbacks published by *Banner of Truth*

Bolton, *The True Bounds of Christian Freedom*

Boston, *Human Nature in its Fourfold State*

Brooks, *An Ark for All God's Noahs in a Gloomy Stormy Day*

Bunyan, *The Pilgrim's Progress, Holy War*

Charnock, *The Existence and Attributes of God*

Coxe, *Covenant Theology: From Adam to Christ*

Erskine, *Law-Death, Gospel-Life*

Fisher, *The Marrow of Modern Divinity*

Marshall, *The Gospel Mystery of Sanctification*

Owen, *Communion With God, The Mortification of Sin,
The Death of Death in the Death of Christ*

Watson, *The Beatitudes*

PASTORAL MINISTRY

Ascol ed., *Dear Timothy*

Borgman, *My Heart for Thy Cause*

Dever, *IX Marks of a Healthy Church*

Lloyd-Jones, *Preaching and Preachers*

Moore, *Good Christians, Good Husbands?*

Packer, *Evangelism and the Sovereignty of God*

Spurgeon, *All Round Ministry, Lectures to my Students*

BIOGRAPHIES

Anderson, *To the Golden Shore: The Life of Adoniram
Judson*

Bainton, *Here I Stand: A Life of Martin Luther*

Edwards ed., *The Diaries of David Brainard*

Logic on Fire (Video biography of Martin Lloyd-Jones)

Luther (Video biography of Martin Luther)

Marsden, *Jonathan Edwards*

Murray, *D. Martin Lloyd-Jones (Two Volume set from
Banner of Truth)*

Nettles, *Living by Revealed Truth* (CH Spurgeon)

Parker, *Calvin*

OTHER IMPORTANT WORKS

Bavinck, *Reformed Dogmatics*

Mueller, *Post Reformation Reformed Dogmatics*

Packer, *Knowing God*

Vos, *Biblical Theology*

Winslow, *The Declension and Revival of Personal Religion in the Soul*

Made in the USA
Middletown, DE
07 July 2019